Unicorn Letters and Numbers Tracing

A

Apple

A
a

B
Ball

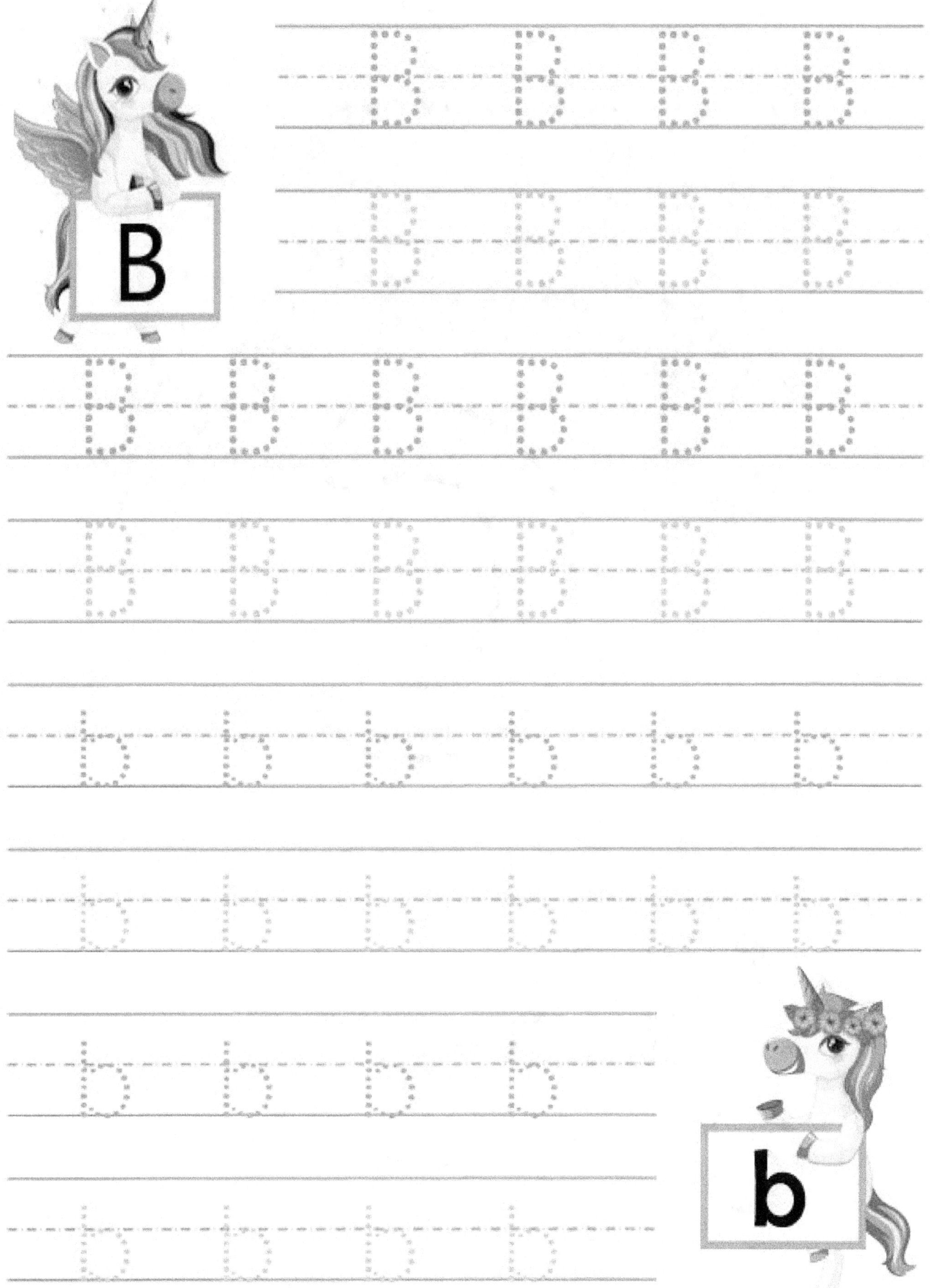
B
b

C

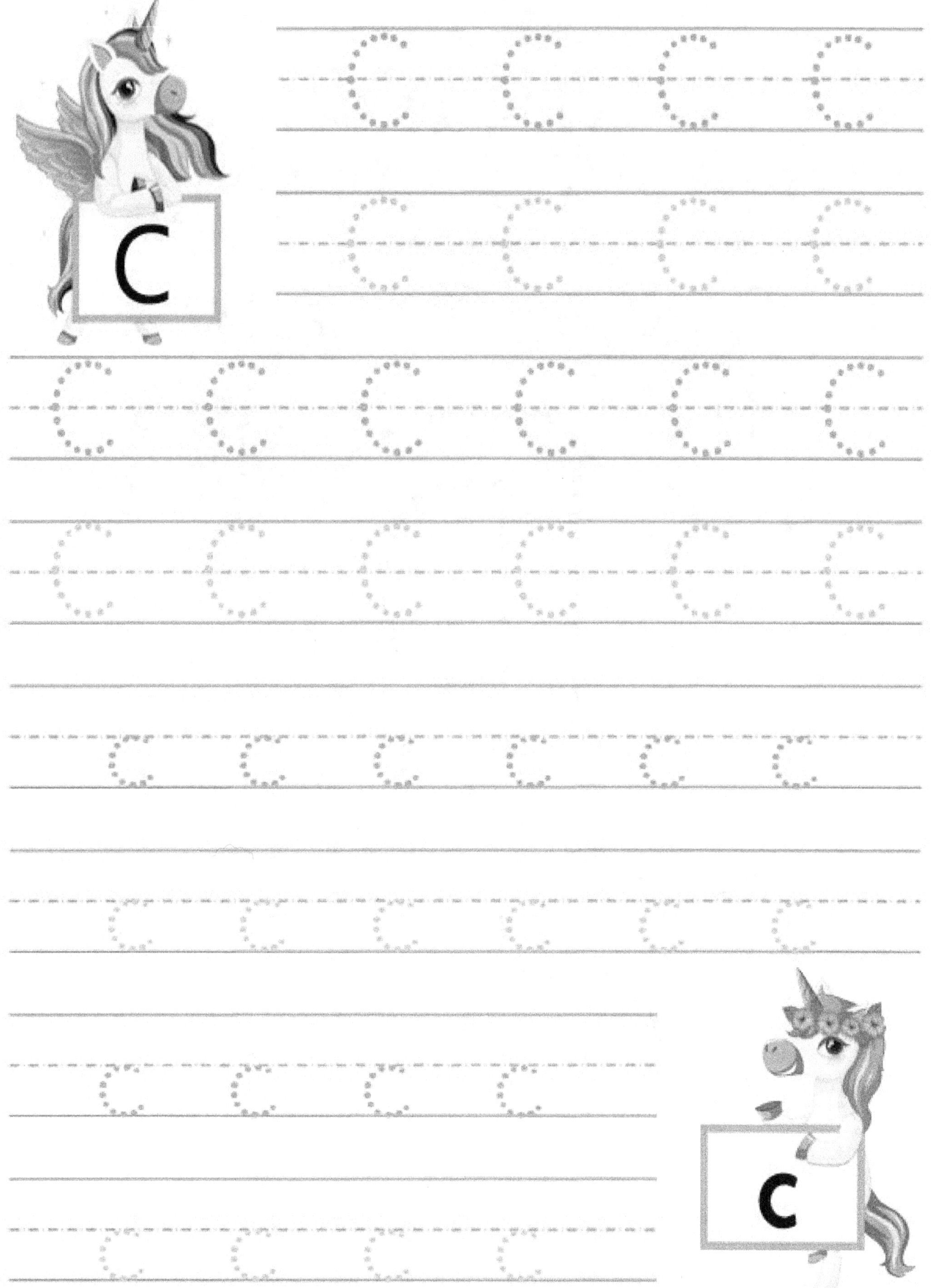
C
c

D
Dolphin

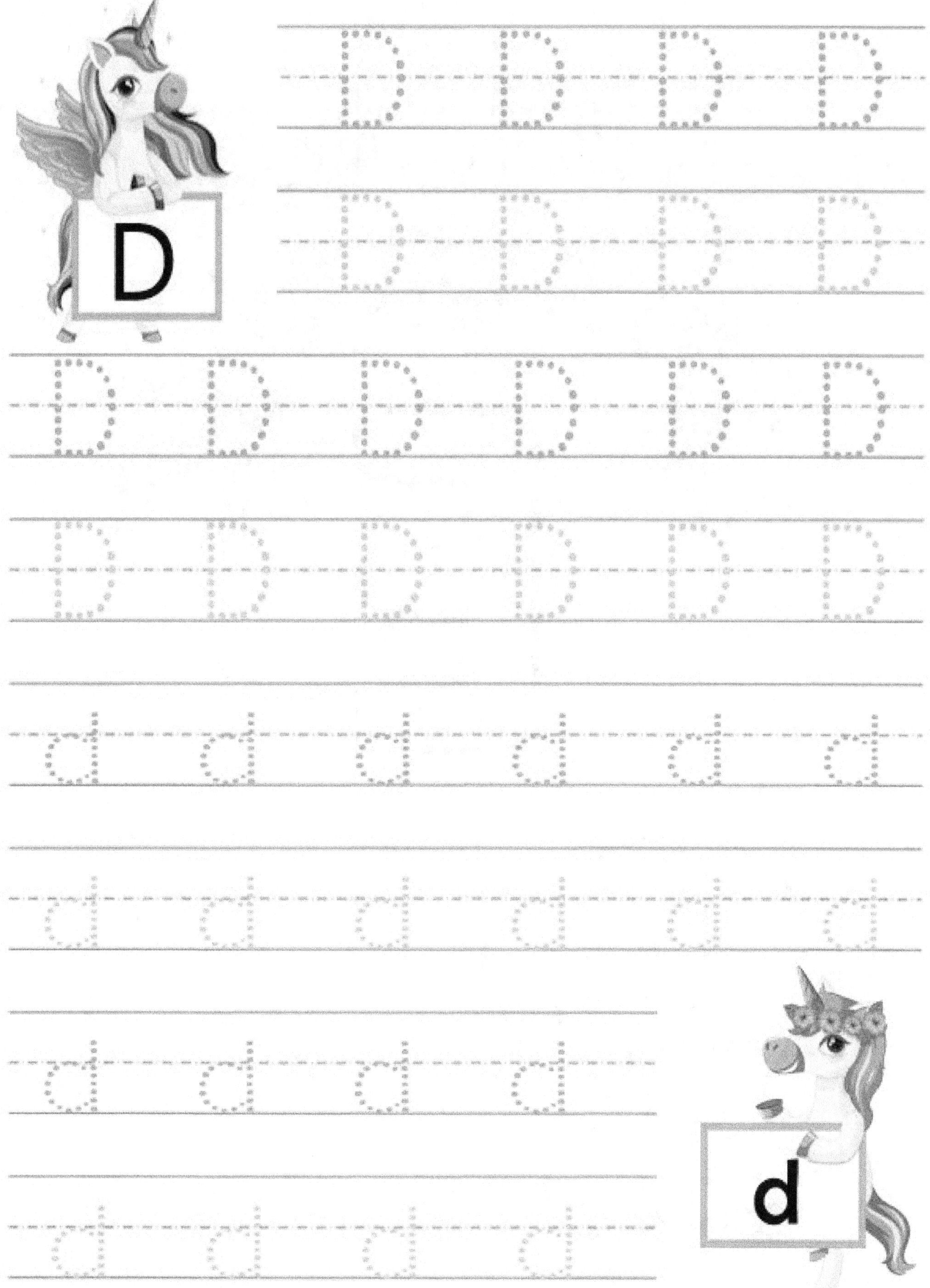
D
d

E

Elephant

E
e

F
Frog

F

f

G
Girl

G
g

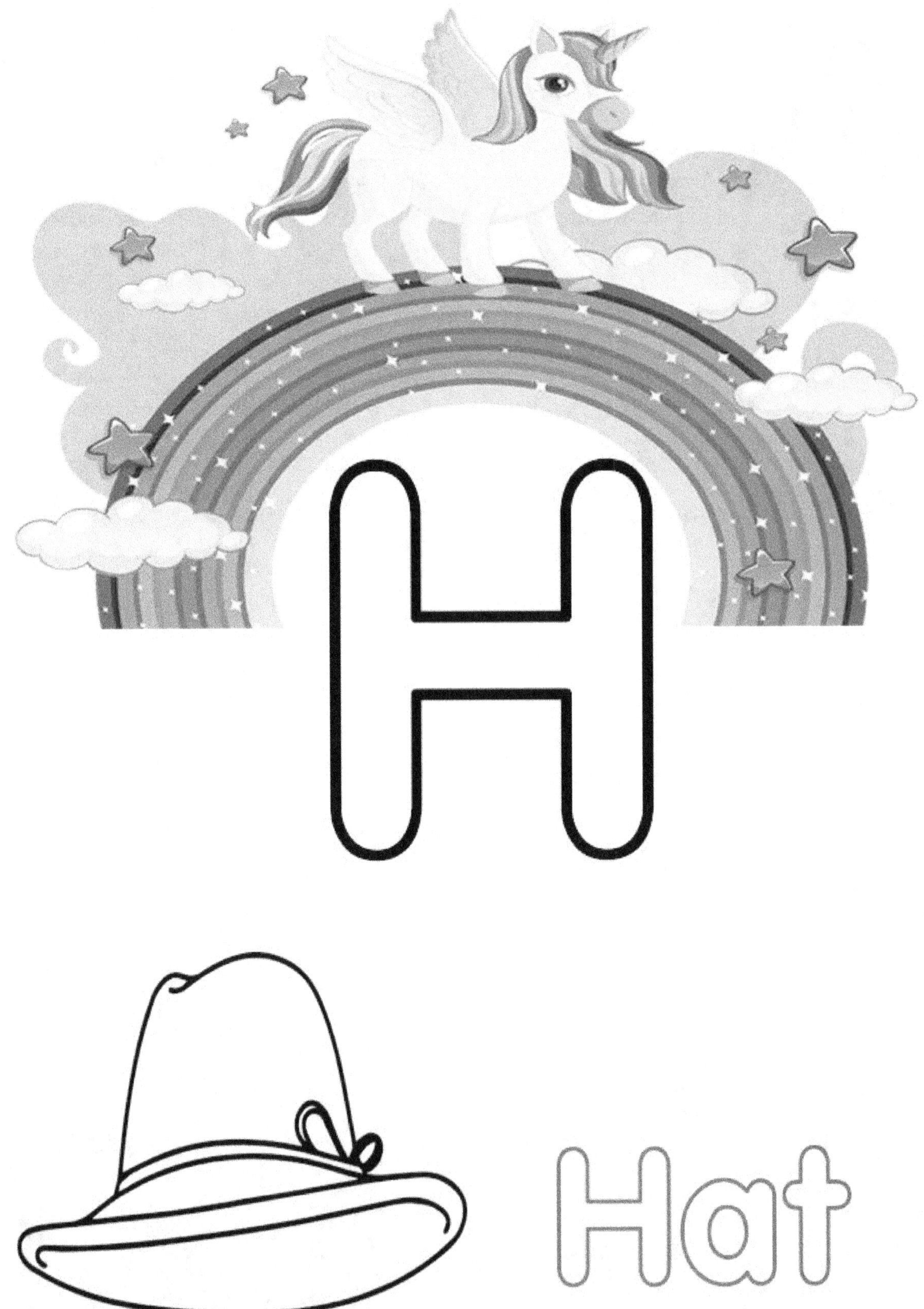

Hat

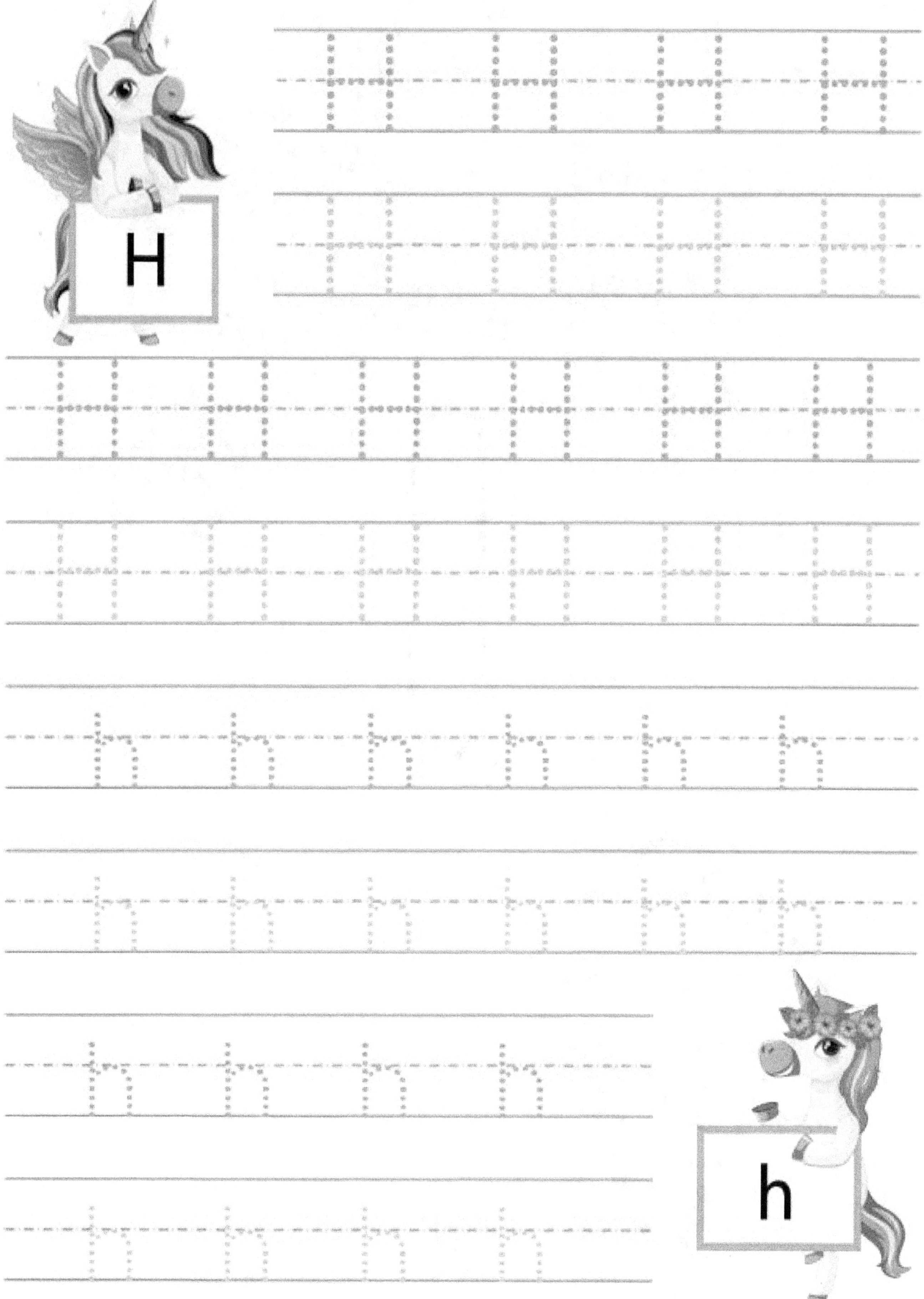
H
h

I
Ice cream

I

i

J
Juice

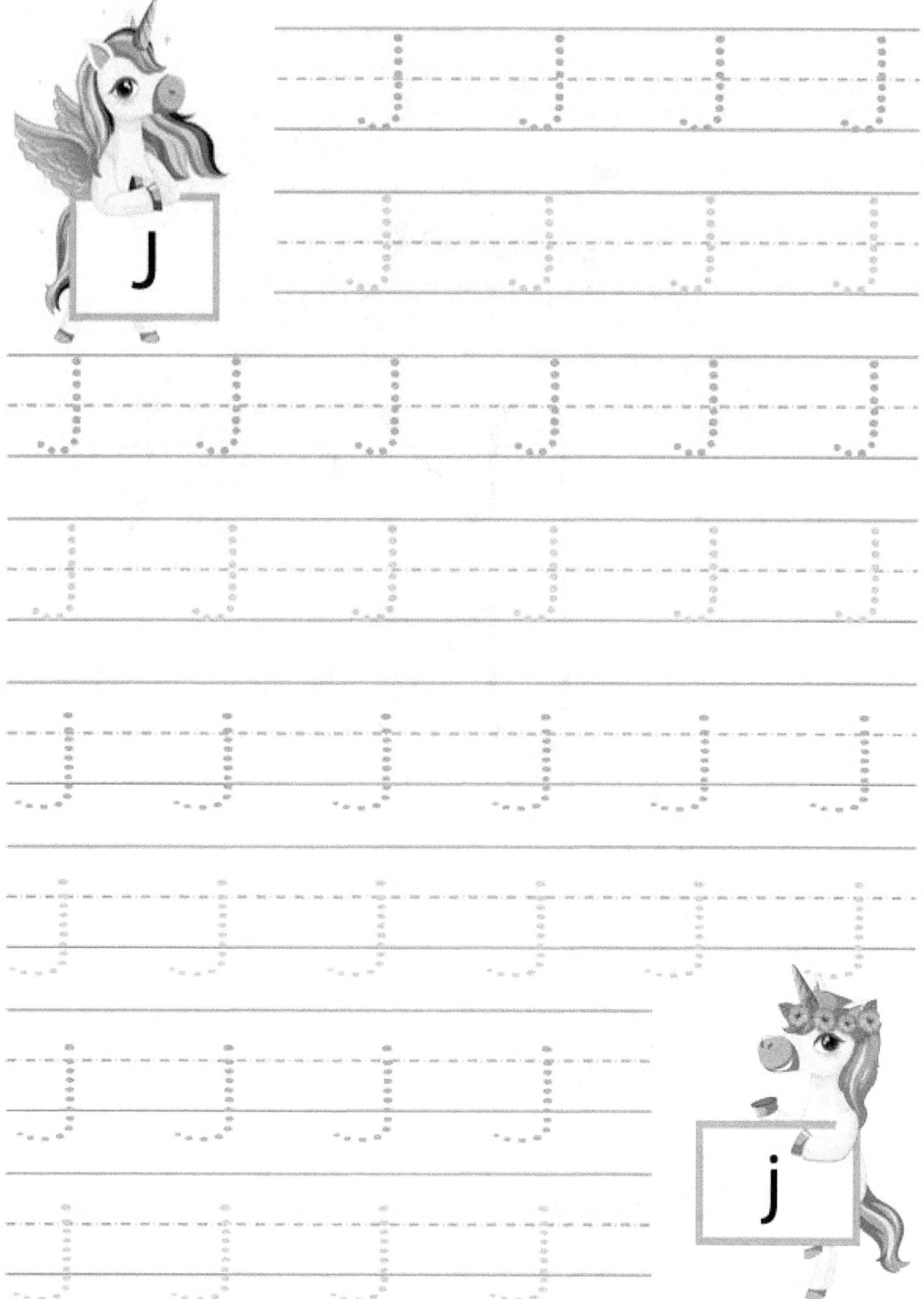

J
j

K

Kangaroo

K
k

L
Lion

L

l

M
Monkey

M
m

Necklace

N
n

O
Octopus

O
o

P
Penguin

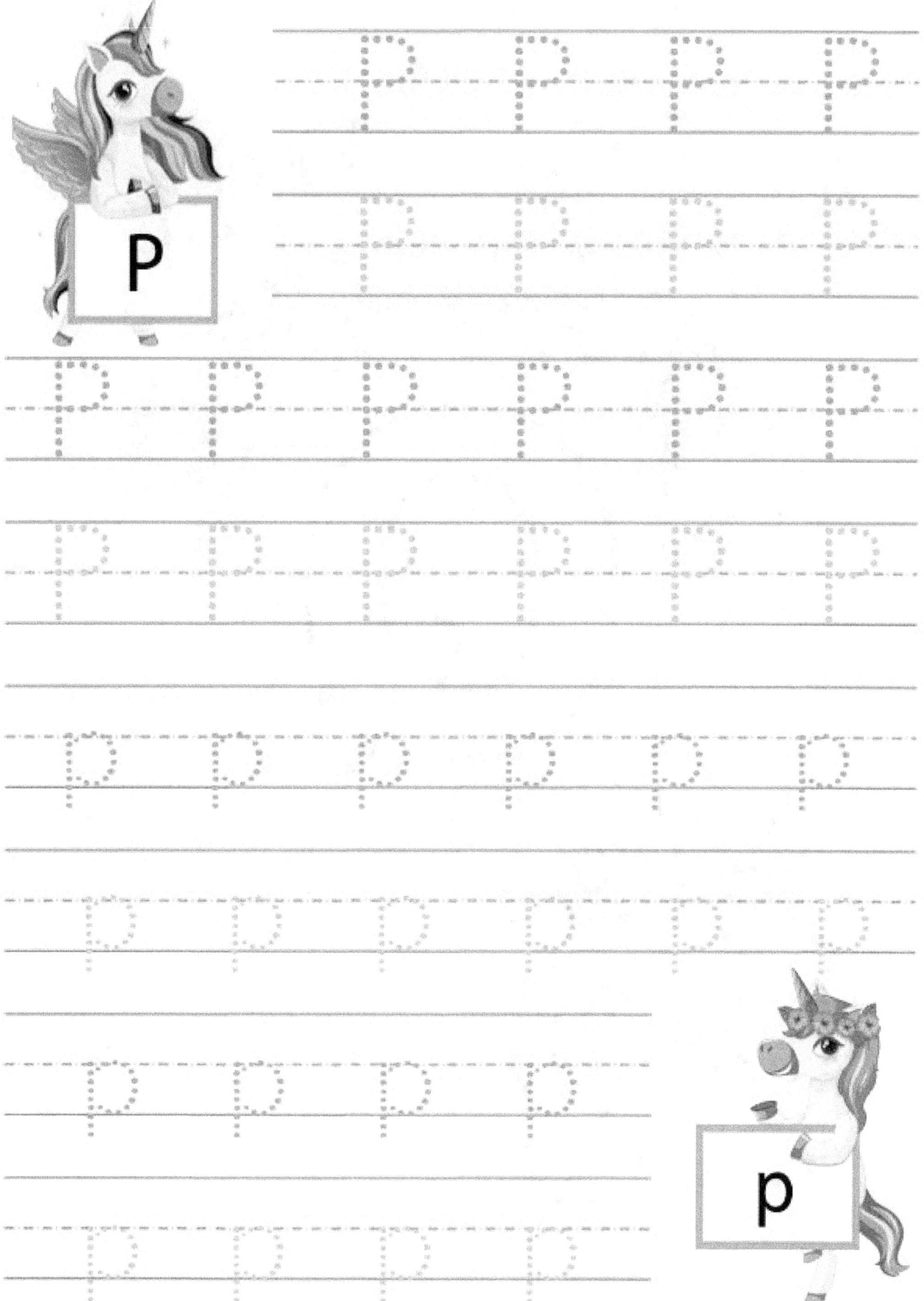
P
p

Q
Queen

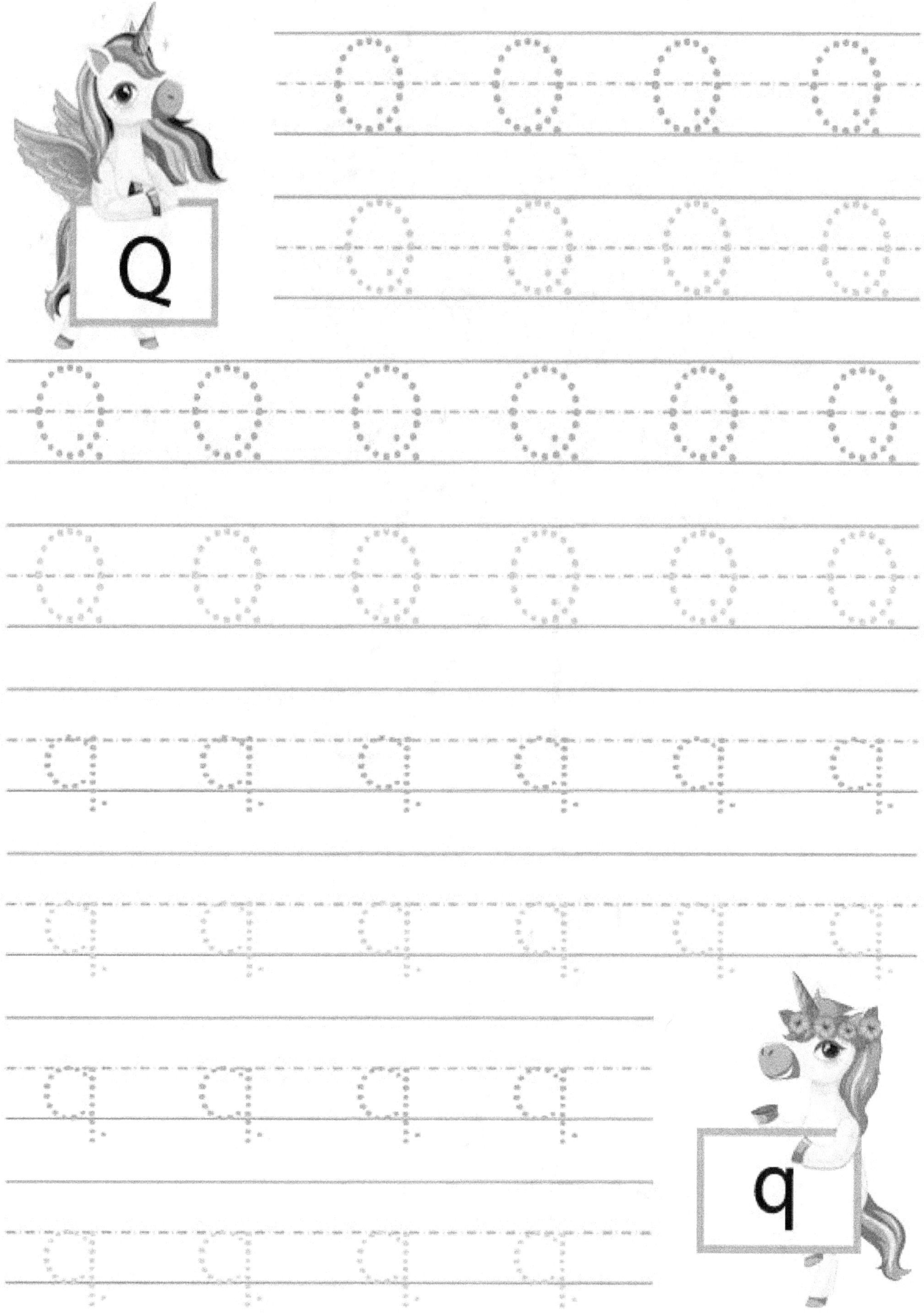
Q
q

R

Rabbit

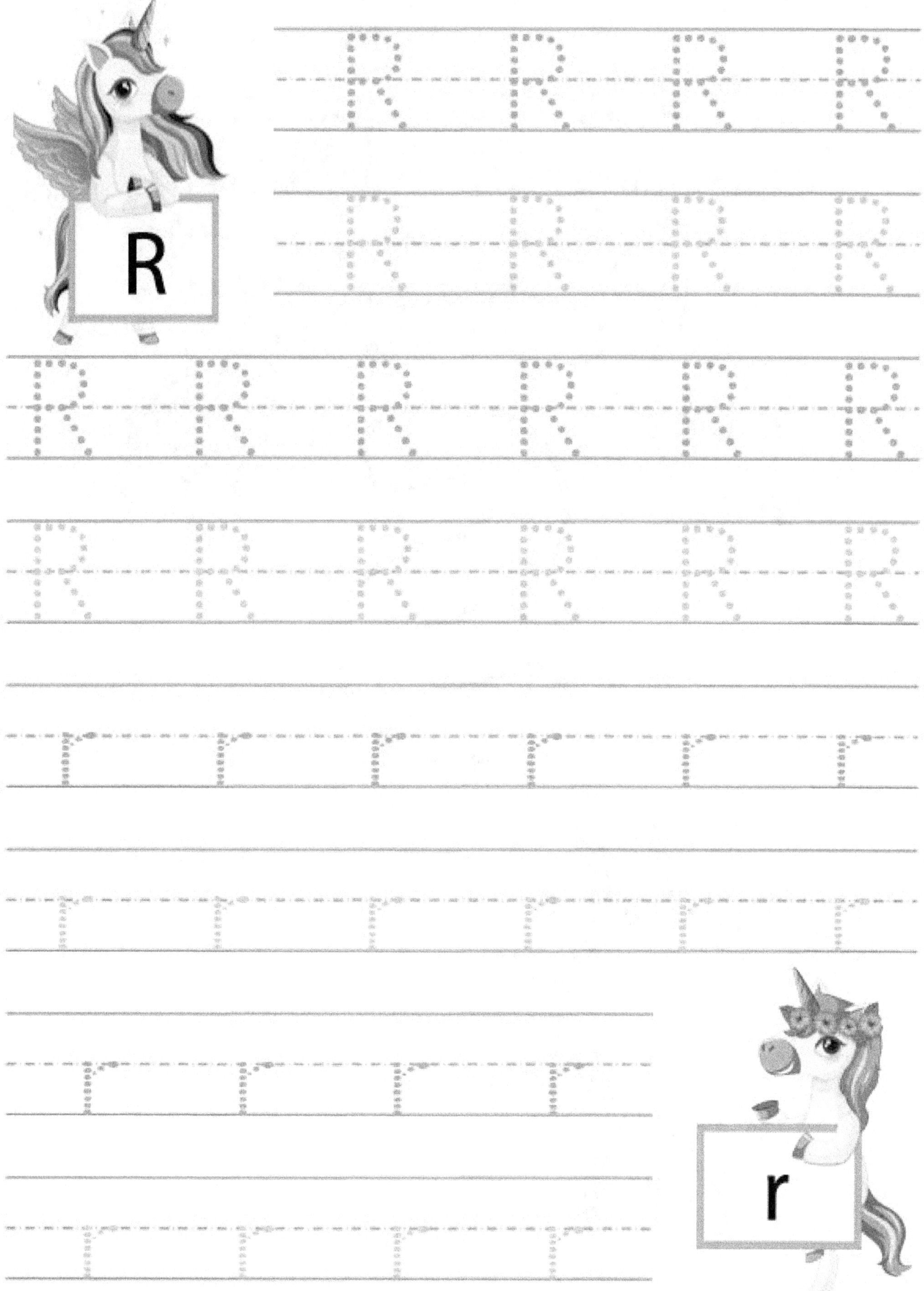
R
r

S
Sun

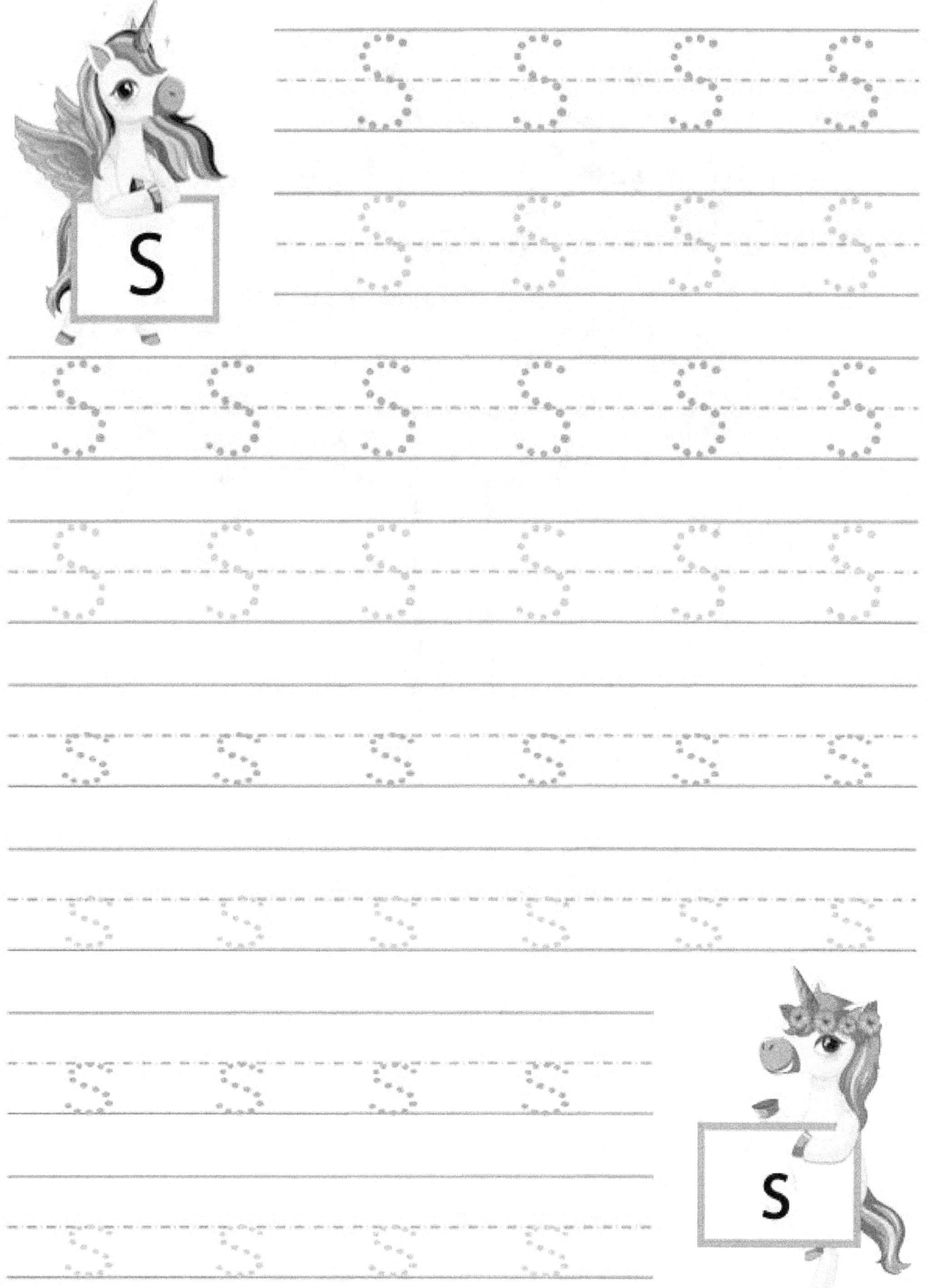
S
s

T
Turtle

T

t

U
Umbrella

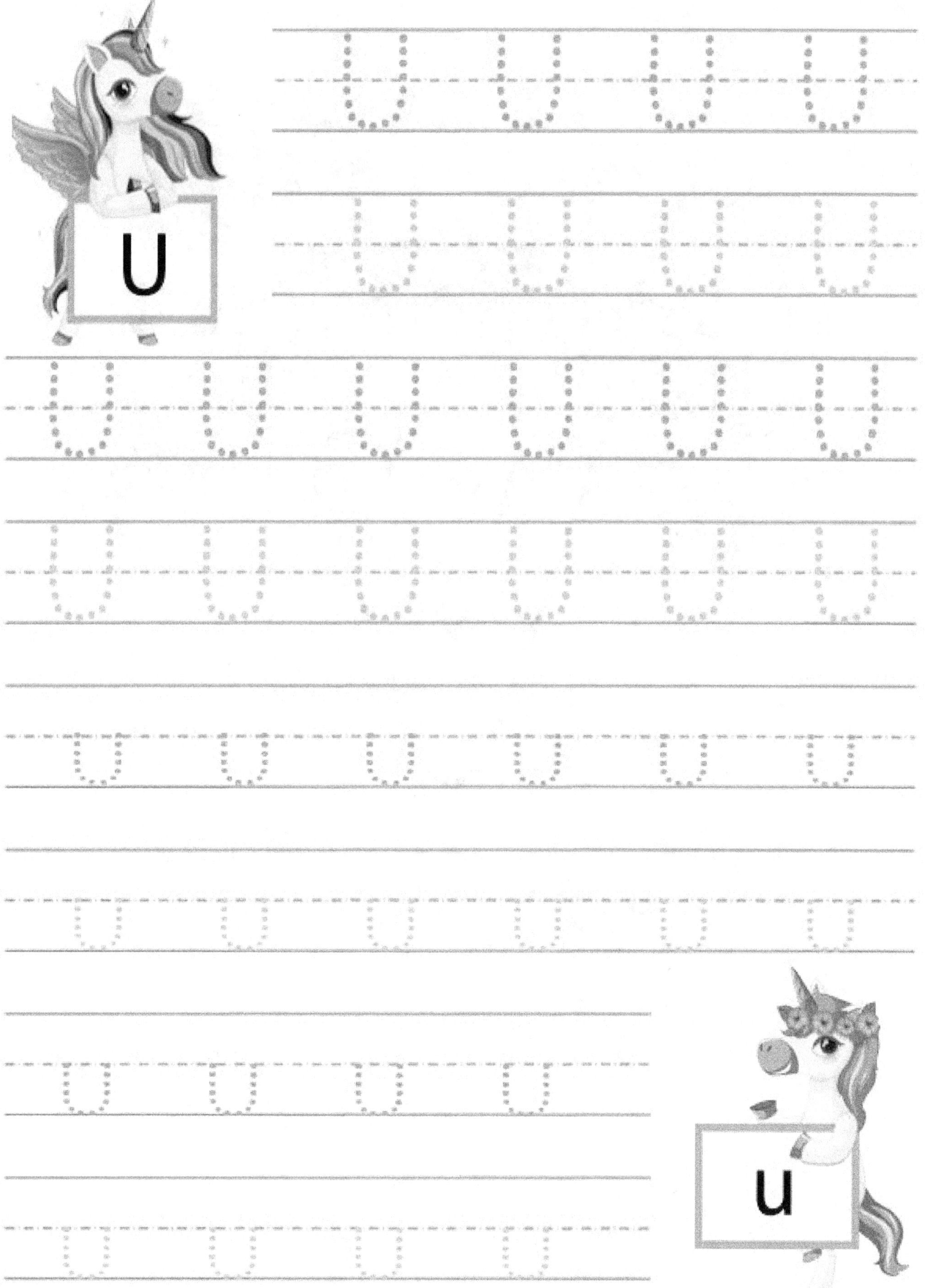
U
u

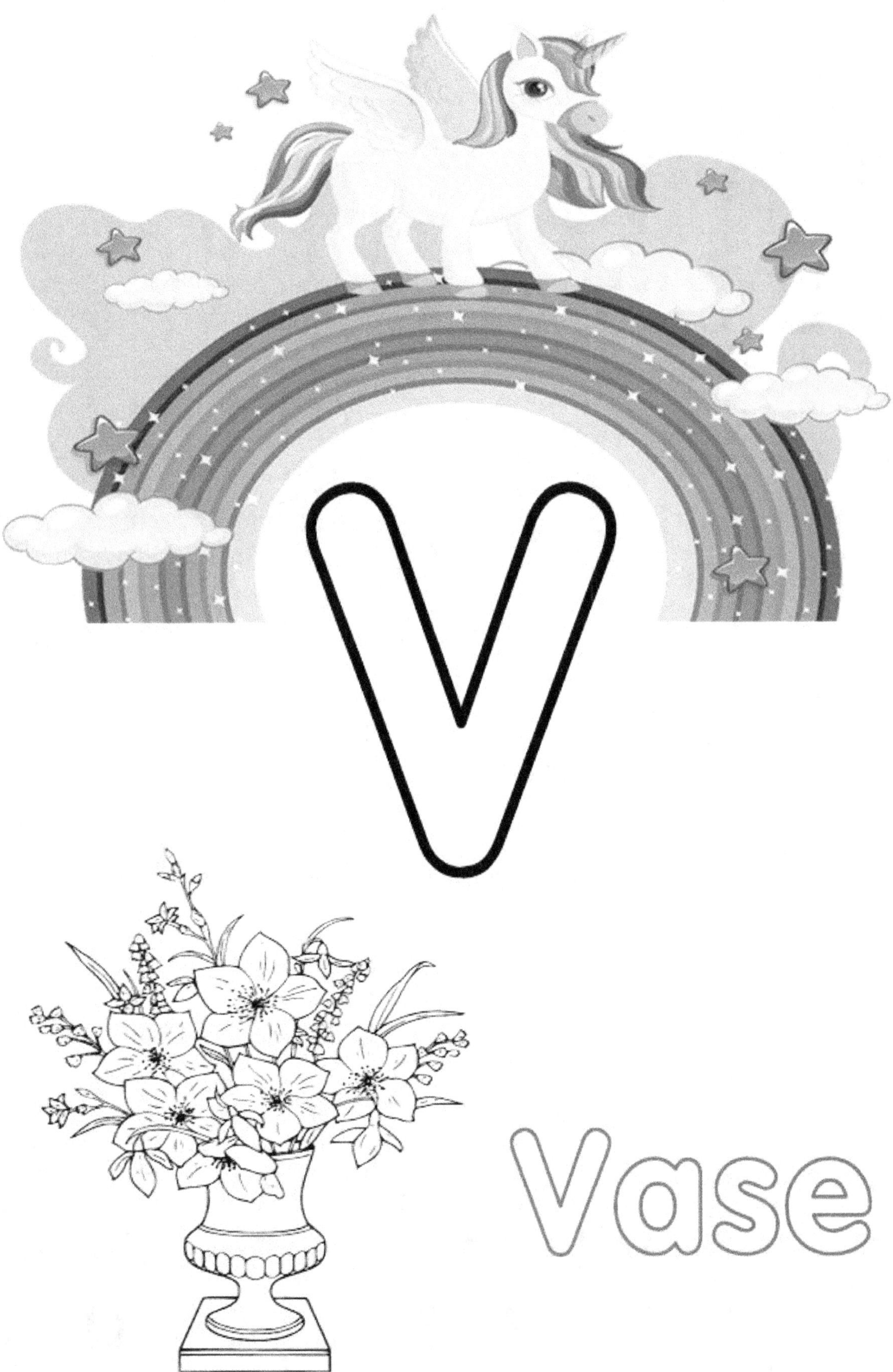
V
Vase

V
v

W

Windmill

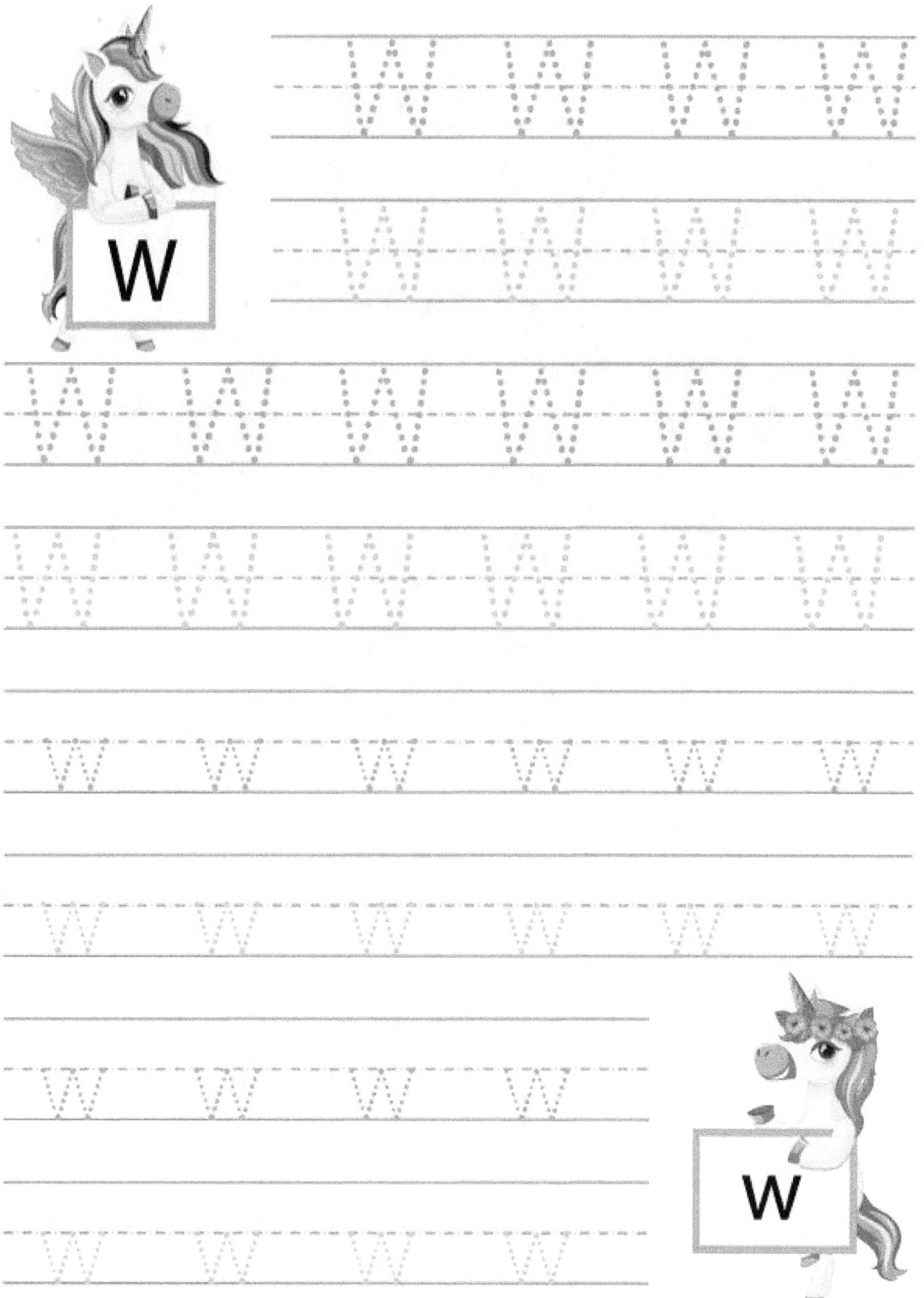
W
w

X
Xylophone

X
x

Y
Yogurt

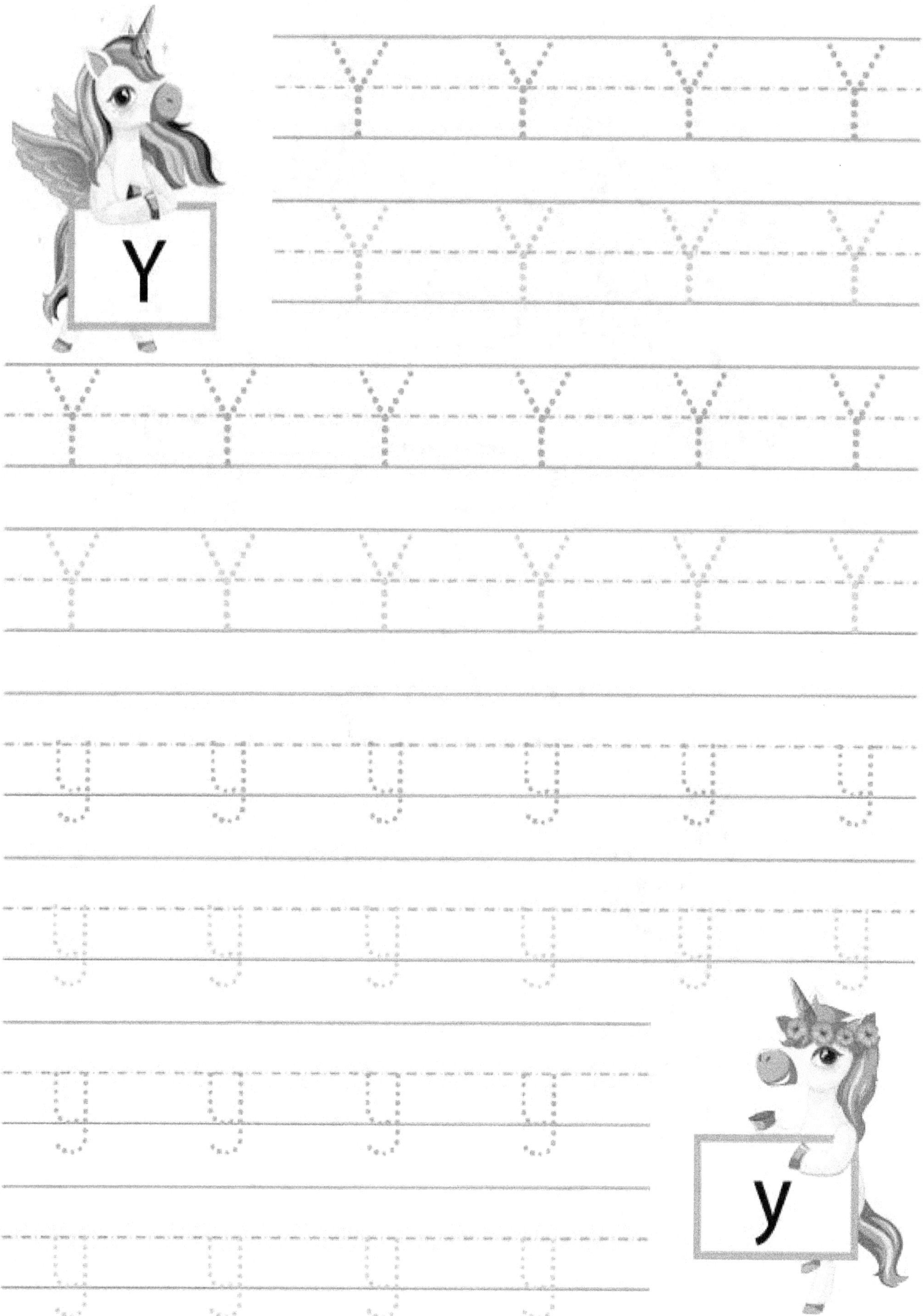
Y
y

Z
Zebra

z
z

1
3
2
5
4

6
8
7
10
9

1

One

1

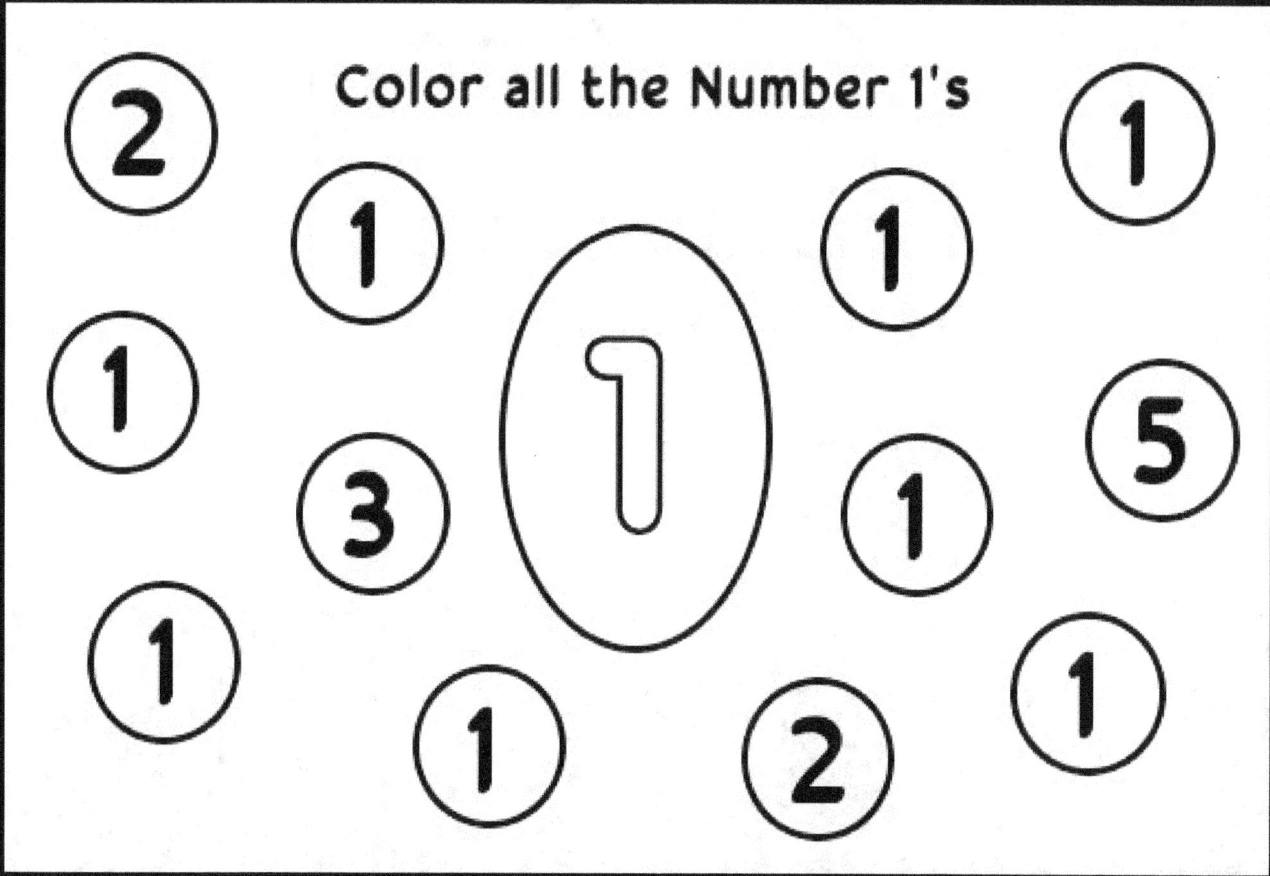

Two

2

Three

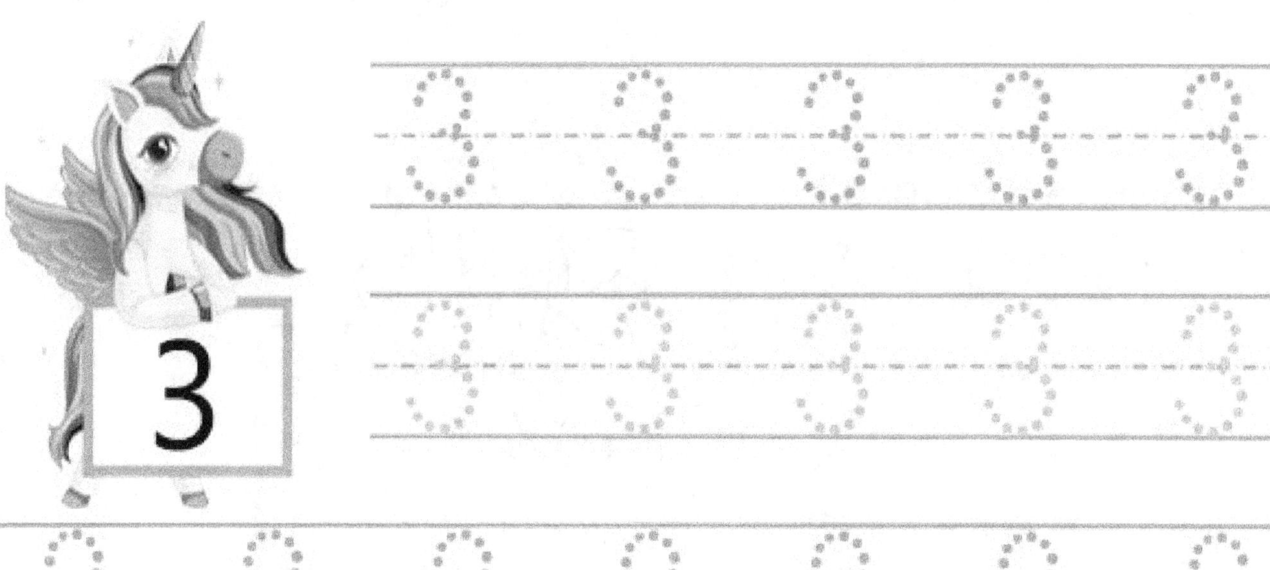

Color all the Number 3's

3 2 3 3 1 3 5 3 1 3 8 2 3

4

Four

4

Five

5

Color all the Number 5's

5 3 2 2 1 5 5 5 1 5 8 7 5

Six

6

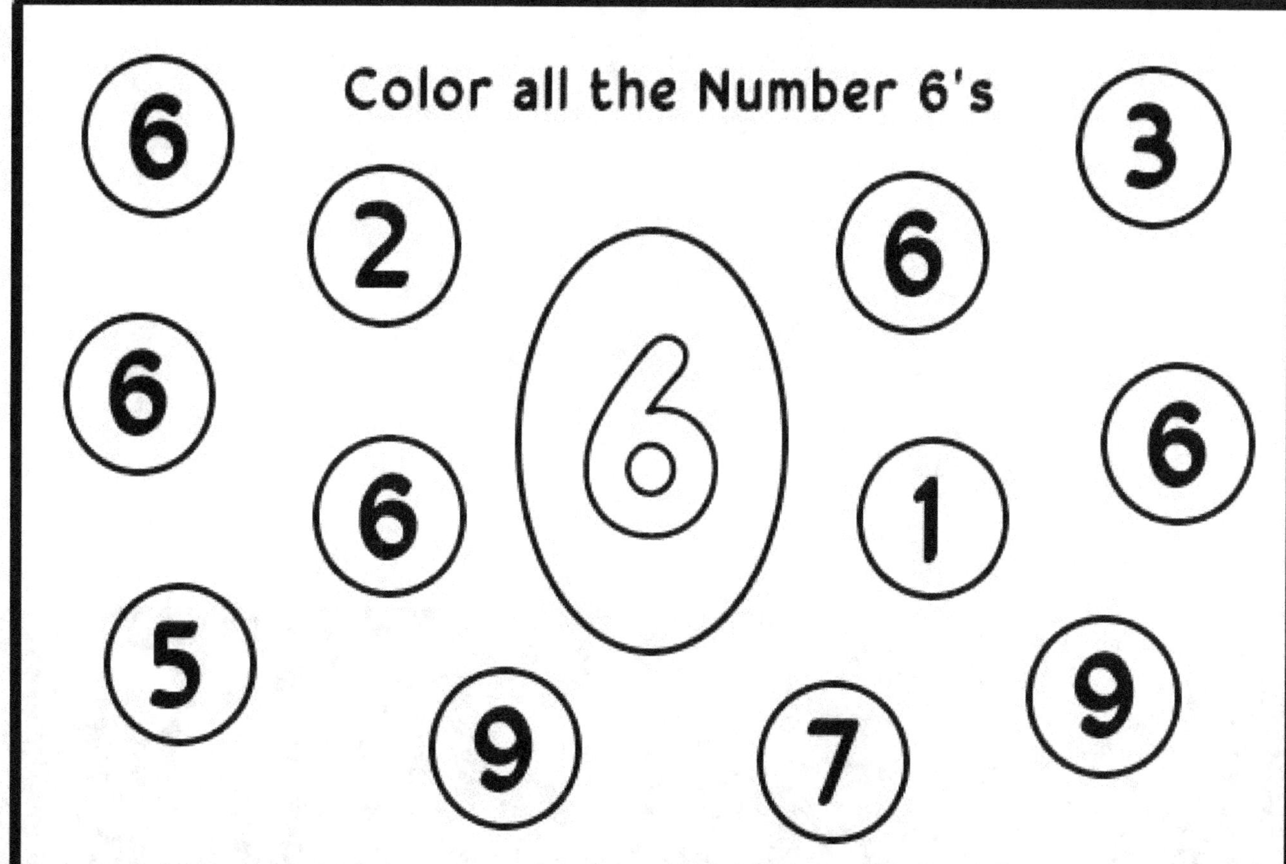
Color all the Number 6's
6
2
6
3
6
6
6
1
6
5
9
7
9

Seven

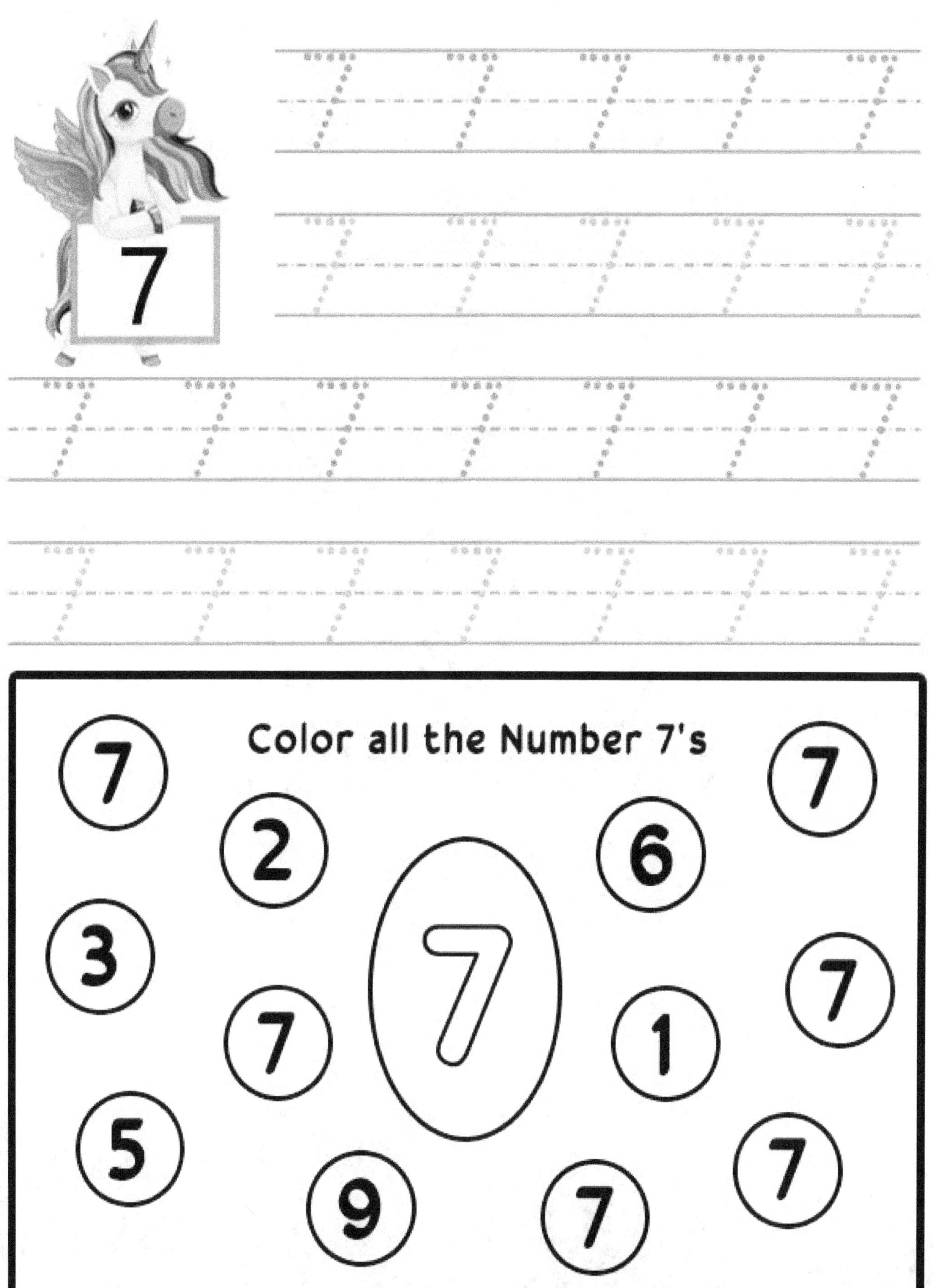
7
Color all the Number 7's
7
2
6
7
3
7
7
7
1
5
7
9
7

Eight

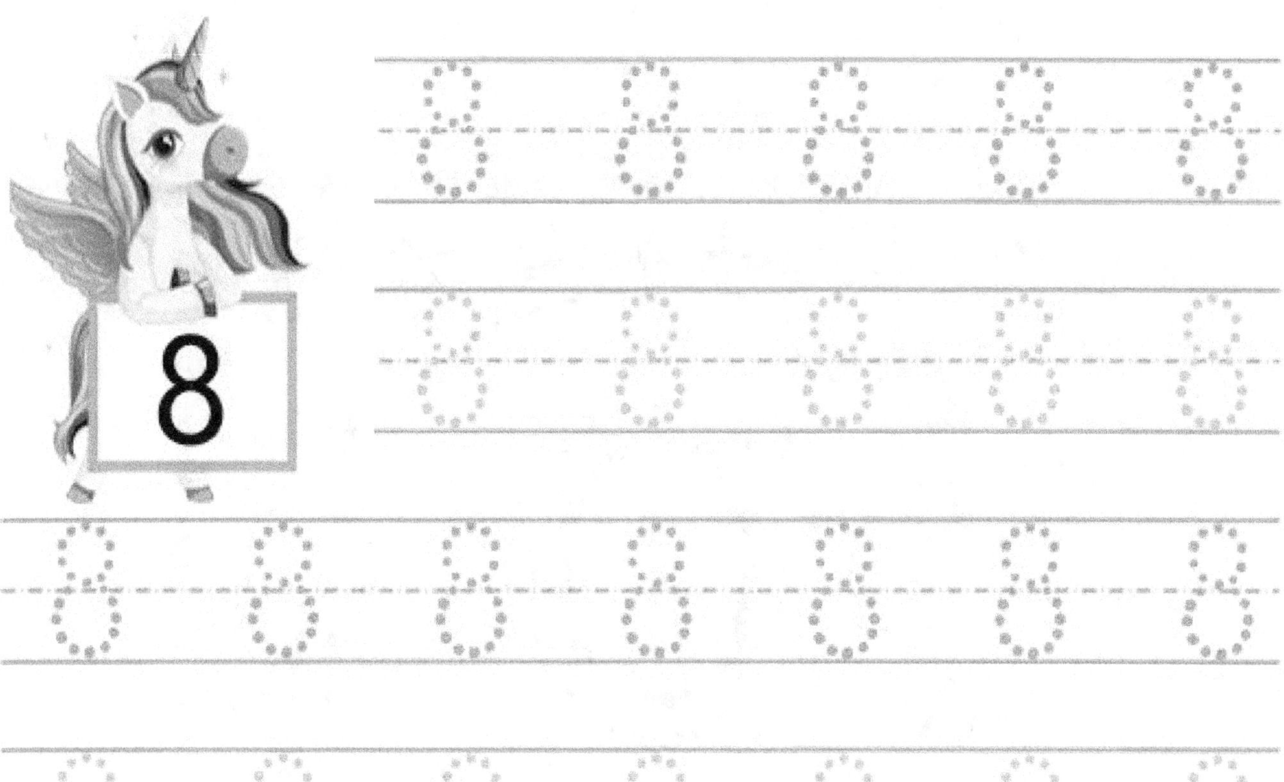

Color all the Number 8's

8 8 6 3 8 8 8 1 5 8 9 7

Nine

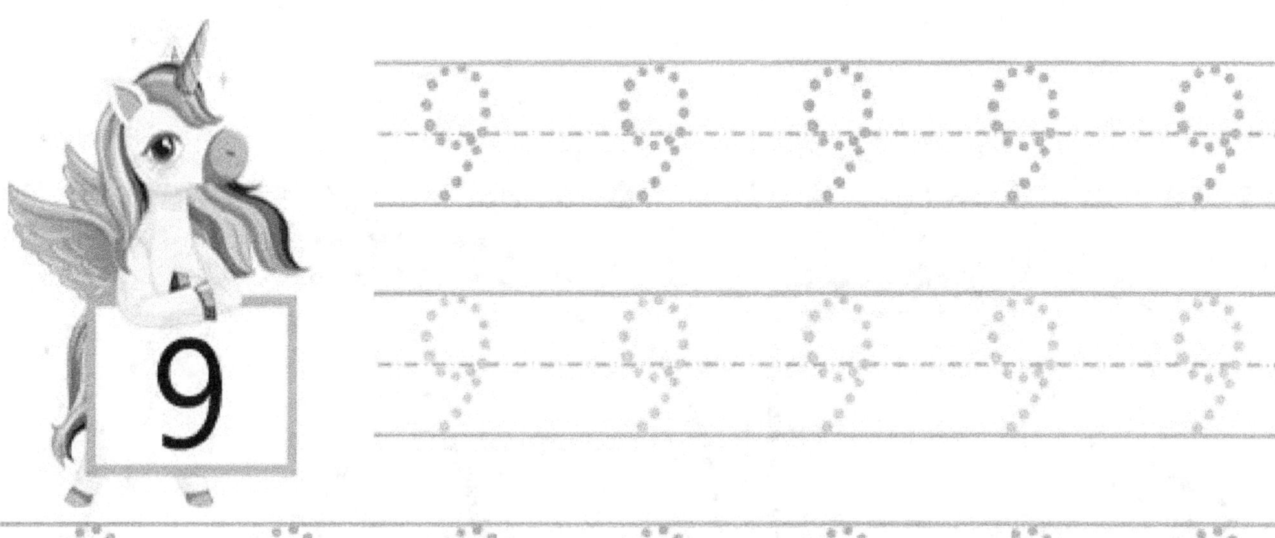

Color all the Number 9's

9 8 6 9 3 9 6 1 9 9 9 7 8 9

Ten

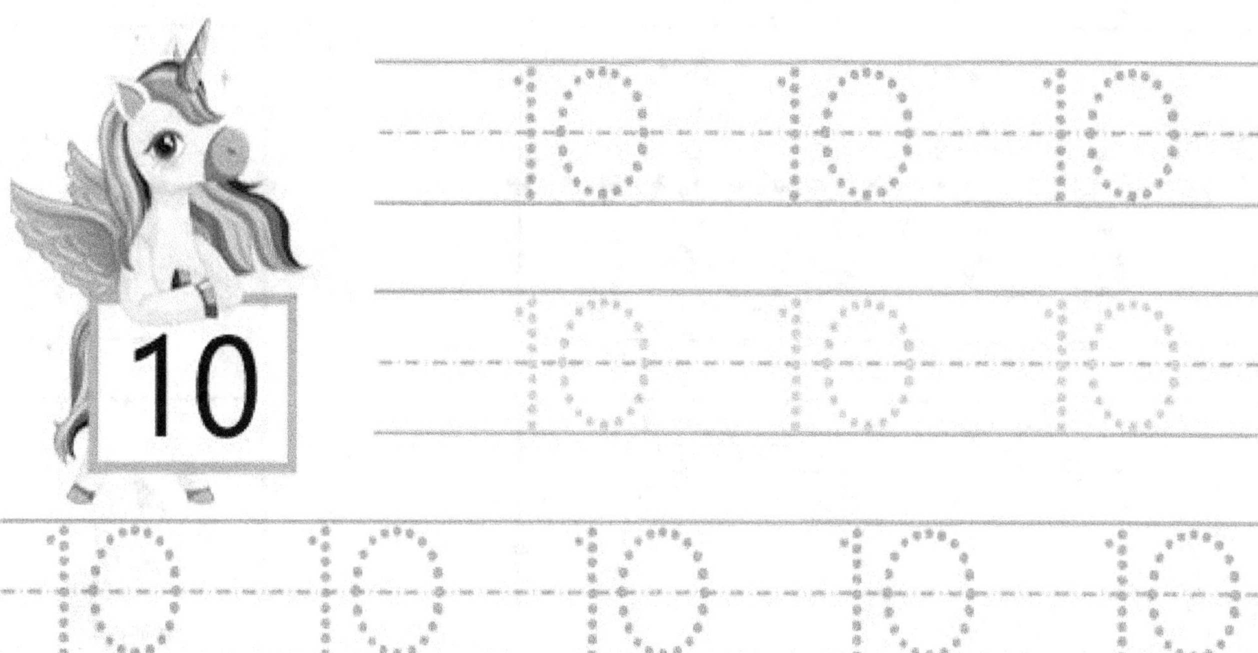

Color all the Number 10's

10

9

8

6

3

10

10

10

1

1

10

10

7

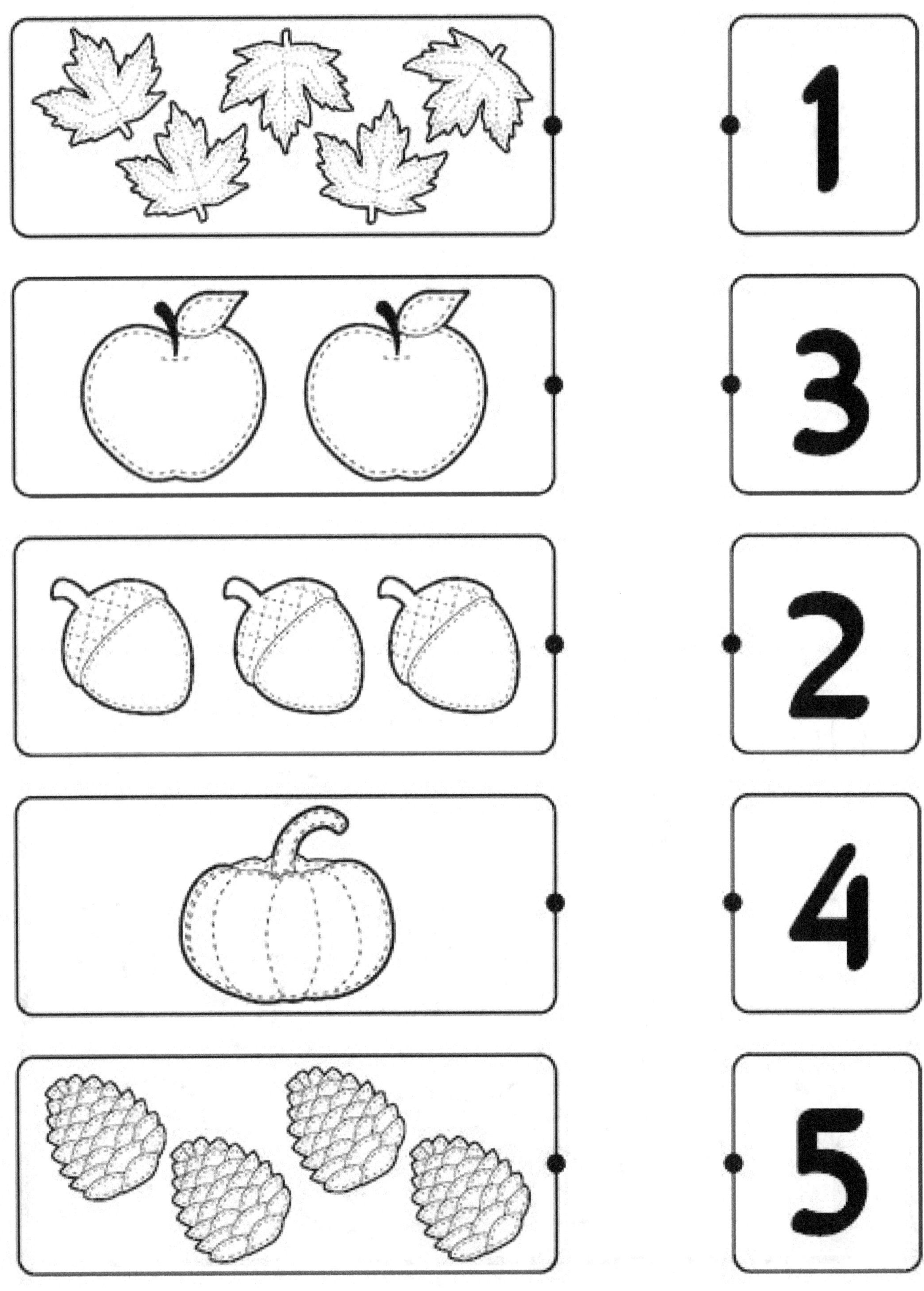
1
3
2
4
5

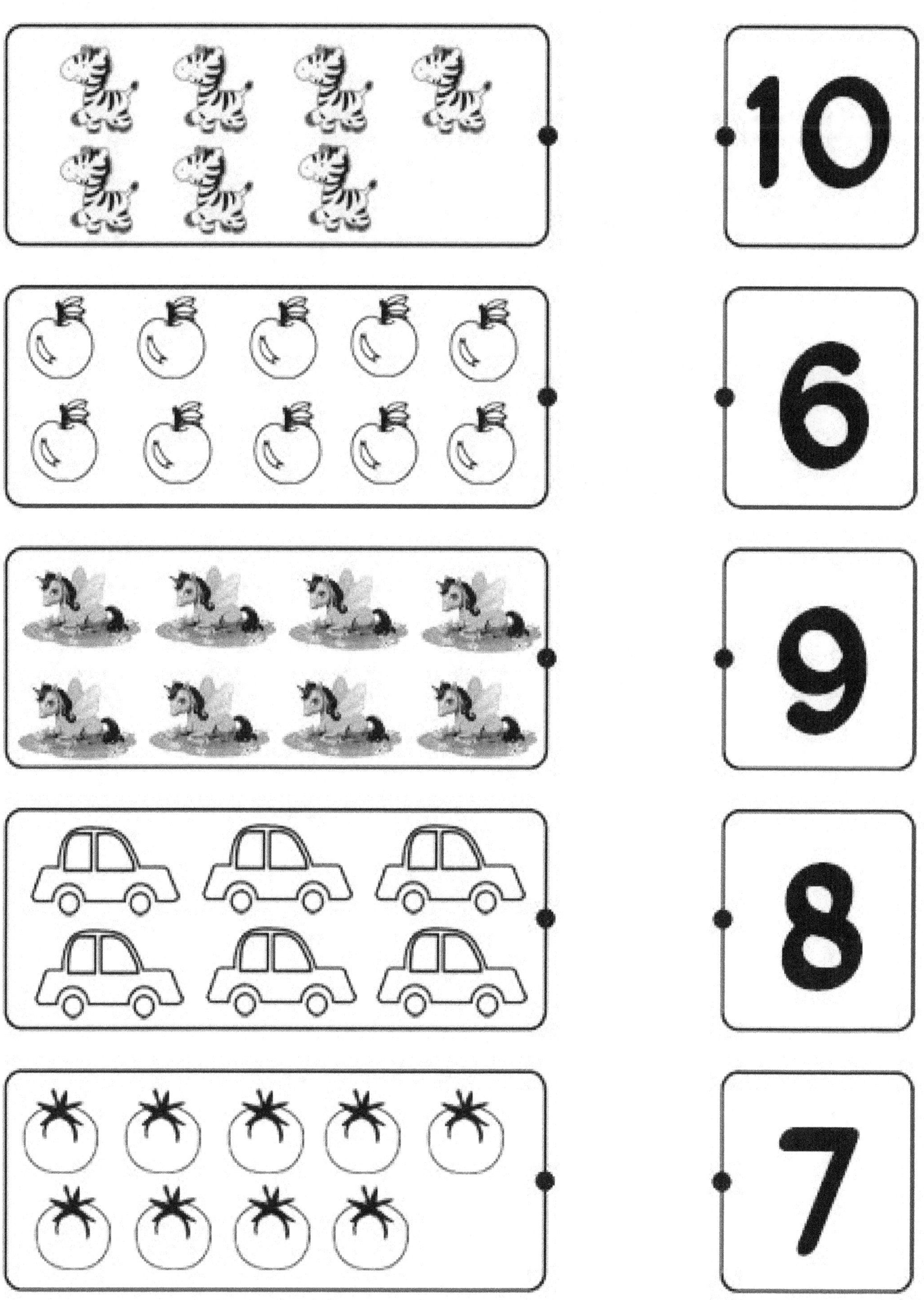
10
6
9
8
7

www.ingramcontent.com/pod-product-compliance
Lightning Source LLC
Chambersburg PA
CBHW081153130726
47996CB00009B/3104

* 9 7 9 8 5 6 6 9 5 5 8 5 8 *